Accompanied by Angels

Accompanied by Angels

POEMS OF THE INCARNATION

Luci Shaw

William B. Eerdmans Publishing Company

Grand Rapids, Michigan / Cambridge, U.K.

Bl, Eerd. 7/06 15.00

Published 2006 by
Wm. B. Eerdmans Publishing Co.
255 Jefferson Ave. S.E., Grand Rapids, Michigan 49503 /
P.O. Box 163, Cambridge CB3 9PU U.K.

Printed in the United States of America

10 09 08 07 06   7 6 5 4 3 2 1

Library of Congress Cataloging-in-Publication Data

Shaw, Luci.
    Accompanied by angels: poems of the Incarnation / Luci Shaw.
      p.   cm.
    ISBN-10: 0-8028-2987-2 / ISBN-13: 978-0-8028-2987-0 (pbk.: alk. paper)
    1. Christian poetry, American.   I. Title.

  PS3569.H384A25 2006
  811'.54 — dc22

                        2006008540

www.eerdmans.com

Contents

Arrival

Living

Dying

Risen

Introduction

Winter. Toronto in the 1940s. I was ten or eleven. It was bleak and dark, with heavy snow, but I was feeling exhilarated by the thought of the coming season of gifts and secrets, of carols and decorated fir trees and colored lights along the eaves — in my young heart it was clearly the time to begin work on Christmas cards.

I determined that my Advent greetings would all be hand-crafted. Laboriously I drew, one by one, pen-and-ink pictures of deer or holly or candles, or I cut and pasted shapes of snow-covered roofs on green construction paper. My Christmas card list was short, of necessity—school friends and family and overseas relatives—but creating something personal and fresh gave me such delight that I've continued the habit the rest of my life.

With the early drawings came short lyrics like this:

Our house is open, Lord, to Thee.
Come in and share our Christmas tree!
We've made each nook and corner bright,
Circled with Christmas candlelight.

But light that never goes away
Is Thine alone, Lord Jesus. Stay,
Shine in our hearts, our Christmas Cheer,
And fill each niche of our New Year.

Now, over sixty years later, the list of Advent poems that I
have shared as greetings to friends has grown long, with a lon-
ger list of addressees—sometimes as many as five hundred. For
many years I collaborated with artists better than I to design the
cards and illustrations—people like Timothy Botts and Kathy
Lay Burrows and Erica Grimm-Vance. Though I still write a per-
sonal note in each before I take them to the post office, I no lon-
ger craft each card by hand. My computer and our local printer
have eased the process. But it is still a great joy to reach out to
friends and colleagues with my own message at Christmas.
Somehow such a greeting assumes more reality and personal
significance in my mind than a computer-generated image or a
store-bought greeting, attractive as those often are.

The poems in *Accompanied by Angels* have found their way
into church bulletins, anthologies of Christmas readings, liter-
ary journals, and other people's Christmas cards. Many of
these poems have also appeared in other collections of my po-
etry, but here, for the first time, I've drawn them all together
between the covers of a single book, and arranged them in
what seemed to me to reflect the chronological order of the life
of Jesus. The annunciation, birth, life, death, resurrection, and

ascension of Christ all come into play in these poems as they attempt to read between the lines of the scriptural accounts. Using the lens of what C. S. Lewis called "the baptized imagination," I've endeavored to enter the realities of the life of the Messiah, the Anointed One, his family and followers, the friends and enemies he encountered during his human life on our planet.

The conditions of Christ's life were often harsh, ominous, and dark with foreshadowing. The merriment and celebration that we associate with the Christmas season were absent from Jesus' life, in the mean circumstances of his birth, in his controversial teachings on topics like personal sacrifice and service. The difficulties of his own life journey toward Gethsemane and Golgotha often get ignored in our Advent church services, and political correctness has attempted to tone down public expressions of our joy in the Incarnation and the Resurrection.

Yet the meanings behind the events, settings, and relationships in our Savior's life are perhaps as important to us today as the narrative descriptions found in the biblical accounts in the prophets and the Gospels.

I'm hoping you will not regard this simply as "a Christmas book," but will see it as a source for reflection and thanksgiving throughout the year. Jesus' life has been celebrated and depicted through the centuries in many forms of art, drama, and literature. Like all art, these poems are only "hints and guesses." But perhaps they will suggest some new possibilities and give you some fresh glimpses of the One who came to earth, and who in birth and resurrection was "accompanied by angels."

Bellingham, Washington, 2006   LUCI SHAW

Announcement

The Annunciatory Angel

(detail of Fra Angelico's The Annunciation*)*

The androgynous visitor is dressed
in a rosy fabric thick as pigment, the tunic
blown back by turbulence to expose its lining,
a blue crescent under the right arm. Angels
are said to be genderless, so there's a certain
enigma. A wing, the clue to otherness,
arcs in golden space. We are

at several removes from the reality, reading
between the lines, speculating on Angelico's
speculation. How does an angel look? We are not
Daniel or Zechariah; we have not been shown.
This rendering suggests not celestial power and radiance
but a weight of apprehension; what must be announced
will not be entirely easy news.

Wind is part of the picture, gusts
whipping the robes and body along a stretch
of baroque carpet. Gabriel seems to be
advancing up an incline, laboring with
the imperative of message, hair flattened against scalp,
features tense, hands folded tight to the chest,

agitation or awe — it is hard to tell. We can't see
the heart hammering in the unearthly body,
but the announcement, the cracking open of a space
that encircles earth and heaven, must weigh
like a gold boulder in the belly.

How might it feel (if an archangel has feelings) to bear
this news? Perhaps as confounded as the girl, there
in the corner? We worry that she might faint.
Weep. Turn away, perplexed and fearful
about opening herself. Refuse to let the wind
fill her, to buffet its nine-month seed into her earth.
She is so small and intact. Turmoil will wrench her.

She might say no.

4

". . . for who can endure the day of his coming?"

Malachi 3:2

When an angel
snapped the old thin threads of speech
with an untimely birth announcement,
slit the seemly cloth of an even more blessed
event with shears of miracle,
invaded the privacy of a dream, multiplied
to ravage the dark silk of the sky,
the innocent ears, with swords of sound:
news in a new dimension demanded
qualification. The righteous were
as vulnerable as others. They trembled
for those strong antecedent *Fear nots*,
whether goatherds, virgins, workers
in wood, or holy barren priests.

In our nights
our complicated modern dreams
rarely flower into visions. No contemporary
Gabriel dumbfounds our worship,
or burning, visits our bedrooms.
No signpost satellite hauls us, earthbound
but star-struck, half around the world

with hope. Are our sensibilities too blunt
to be assaulted with spatial power-plays
and far-out proclamations of peace?
Sterile, skeptics, yet we may be broken
to his slow, silent birth, his beginning
new in us. His big-ness may still burst
our self-containment to tell us,
without angels' mouths, *Fear not.*

God knows we need to hear it, now,
when he may shatter, with his most shocking
coming, this proud, cracked place,
and more if, for longer waiting,
he does not.

6

Advent Visitation

Even from the cabin window I sensed the wind's
contagion begin to infect the rags of leaves.
Then the alders gilded to it, obeisant, the way

angels are said to bow, covering their faces with
their wings, not solemn, as we suppose, but
possessed of a sudden, surreptitious hilarity.

When the little satin wind arrived,
I felt it slide through the cracked-open door
(A wisp of prescience? A change in the weather?),

and after the small push of breath — You
entering with your air of radiant surprise,
I the astonished one.

These still December mornings
I fancy I live in a clear envelope of angels
like a cellophane womb. Or a soap bubble,

the colors drifting, curling. Outside
everything's tinted rose, grape, turquoise,
silver — the stones by the path, the skin of sun

on the pond ice, at night the aureola of
a pregnant moon, like me, iridescent,
almost full-term with light.

Announcement

Yes, we have seen the studies, sepia strokes
across yellowed parchment, the fine detail
of hand and breast and the fall of cloth —
Michelangelo, Caravaggio, Titian, El Greco,
Rouault — each complex madonna plotted at last
on canvas, layered with pigment, like the final
draft of a poem after thirty-nine roughs.

But Mary, virgin, had no sittings, no chance
to pose her piety, no novitiate for body or
for heart. The moment was on her unaware:
the Angel in the room, the impossible demand,
the response without reflection. Only one
word of curiosity, echoing Zechariah's *How?*
yet innocently voiced, without request for proof.
The teen head tilted in light, the hand
trembling a little at the throat, the candid
eyes, wide with acquiescence to shame and glory —
"Be it unto me as you have said."

Magnificat

I am singing my Advent anthem to you, God: How all year
I've felt your thrusts, every sound and sight stabbing
like a little blade — the creak of gulls, the racket
as waves jostle pebbles, the road after rain, shining
like a river, the scrub of wind on the cheek, a flute
trilling — clean as a knife, the immeasurable chants of green,
of sky: messages, announcements. But of what? Who?

Then last Tuesday, a peacock feather (surprise!)
spoke from the grass; Flannery called hers "a genuine
word of the Lord." And I — as startled as Mary, nearly,
at your arrival in her chamber (the invisible
suddenly seen, urgent, iridescent, having put on light
for her regard) — I brim over like her, quickening. I can't
stop singing, thoroughly pregnant with Word!

Salutation

Luke 1:39-45

Framed in light,
Mary sings through the doorway.
Elizabeth's six-month joy
jumps, a palpable greeting,
a hidden first encounter
between son and Son.

10

And my heart turns over
when I meet Jesus
in you.

The Meaning of White Oaks

It is light that tugs,
that teaches each
acorn to defy the pull
down, to interrupt
horizontal space.
And falling, filtering
through the pale green leaves,
it is rain that rises,
then, like a spring
at a sapling's heart.
It is wind that trains,
toughens the wood.
It is time that spreads
the grain in rings —
dark ripples in
a slow pond.

The oaks learn slowly,
well, twisting
up, around, and out,
finding the
new directions of
the old pattern branded
in each branch,

compacting, a wood
dense enough for us
to craft into a crib
for a newborn, a floor
for dancing, a table
for bread and wine,
a door to open,
welcoming daylight.

The Overshadow

". . . the power of the Most High
will overshadow you . . ."

Luke 1:35

When we think of God, and
angels, and the Angel,
we suppose ineffable light.

So there is surprise in the air
when we see him bring to Mary,
in her lit room, a gift of darkness.

What is happening under that
huge wing of shade? In that mystery
what in-breaking wildness fills her?

She is astonished and afraid; even in
that secret twilight she bends her head,
hiding her face behind the curtain

of her hair; she knows that
the rest of her life will mirror
this blaze, this sudden midnight.

Too Much to Ask

It seemed too much to ask
of one small virgin
that she should stake shame
against the will of God.
All she had to hold to, later,
were those soft, inward
flutterings
and the remembered surprise
of a brief encounter — spirit
with flesh.
Who would think it
more than a dream wish?
An implausible, laughable
defense.

And it may seem much
too much to ask me
to be part of the
risky thing —
God's shocking, unconventional,
unheard-of Thing —
to further heaven's hopes
and summon God's glory.

Virgin

As if until that moment
nothing real
had happened since Creation

As if outside the world were empty
so that she and he were all
there was — he mover, she moved upon

As if her submission were the most
dynamic of all works; as if
no one had ever said Yes like that

As if that day the sun had no place
in all the universe to pour its gold
but her small room

Arrival

One

Winter, and very cold,
and the night at
its deepest. The politicians,
as usual, double-tongued.
The town chaotic, teeming
with strangers.
And tonight, as often
in winter, in Bethlehem,
snow is falling.

I always love
how each flake,
torn from the sky,
arrives separately,
without sound, almost
unnoticed in
a flurry of others. How
each one (on a clear
night) lies there glittering
on the swelling breast
of snow, crisp
and intact, as wholly itself
as every radiant star

in a sky sparkling
with galaxies.

How many new
babies tonight
in Judea, coming
like snowflakes?
But plucked,
dazzling, from the
eternal heavens
into time,
tonight is born
The One.

Major Theme to a Minor Tune

The sky is black as an empty heart.
The sky is pierced with stars loud as angels,
and all I can exclaim to myself is *Mirabile!*
This is a time of premonition and sharp surprise,
and scurrying feet.

From the eaves icicles fall and break with
a tinkle like bells.
In the wind dead leaves scatter, spent as straw
in a dull manger.
All I can mutter is *Amen!*
This is a month of frosts, and rebuff,
and questions hard as birth.

Astonishment — a baby
bursts bloody from the womb.
Air spins from his fresh lungs like a word
so that all we can chant — a mass in A minor —
is *Kyrie:*
This is a season of serial visions, and a bodily God,
and a sword in the heart.

A Blessing for the New Baby

Lightly as a falling star, immense, may you
drop into the body of the pure young girl like a seed
into its furrow, entering your narrow home under the shadow
of Gabriel's feathers. May your flesh shape itself within her,
swelling her with shame and glory. May her belly grow
round as a small planet, a bowl of golden fruit.

When you suck in your first breath, and your loud cries
echo through the cave (Blessings on you, little howler!),
may Mary adorn you with tears and caresses like ribbons,
her face glowing, a moon among stars. At her breasts
may you drink the milk of mortality that transforms you,
even more, into one of your own creatures.

And now, as the night of this world folds you in
its brutal frost (the barnyard smell strong as sin),
and as Joseph, weary with unwelcome and relief, his hands
bloody from your birth, spreads his thin cloak
around you both, we doubly bless you, Baby,
as you are acquainted, for the first time, with our grief.

Christmas stars

Blazes the star behind the hill.
Snow stars glint from the wooden sill.
A spider spins her silver still

within your darkened stable shed;
in asterisks her webs are spread
to ornament your manger bed.

Where does a spider find the skill
to sew a star? Invisible,
obedient, she works your will

with her swift silences of thread.
I weave star poems in my head;
the spider, wordless, spins instead.

Descent

Down he came from *up*,
and *in* from *out,*
and *here* from *there.*
A long leap,
an incandescent fall
from magnificent
to naked, frail, small,
through space,
between stars,
into our chill night air,
shrunk, in infant grace,
to our damp, cramped
earthy place
among all
the shivering sheep.

And now, after all,
there he lies,
fast asleep.

I gave this day to God

I gave this day to God when I got up, and look,
look what it birthed! There, up the hill, stood

the apple tree, bronze leaves, its fallen apples
spilling richly down the slope, the way God spilled

his seed into Mary, into us. In her the holy promise
came to rest in generous soil after a long

fall. How often it ends in gravel, or dry dust.
Blackberry patches thorny with distraction. Oh,

I pray my soul will welcome always that small
seed. That I will hail it when it enters me.

I don't mind being grit, soil, dirt, mud-brown,
laced with the rot of old leaves, if only the seed

can find me, find a home and bear a fruit
sweet, flushed, full-fleshed — a glory apple.

Made Flesh

After
the white-hot beam of annunciation
fused heaven with dark earth,
his searing, sharply focused light
went out for a while,
eclipsed in amniotic gloom:
his cool immensity of splendor,
his universal grace,
small-folded in a warm, dim
female space —
the Word stern-sentenced to be
nine months' dumb —
infinity walled in a womb,
until the next enormity —
the Mighty One, after submission
to a woman's pains,
helpless on a barn's bare floor,
first-tasting bitter earth.

Now
I in him surrender
to the crush and cry of birth.
Because eternity
was closeted in time,

he is my open door to forever.
From his imprisonment
my freedoms grow,
find wings. Part of this body,
I transcend this flesh.
From his sweet silence my mouth sings.
Out of his dark I glow.
My life, as his,
slips through death's mesh,
time's bars,
joins hands with heaven,
speaks with stars.

Breath

When, in the cavern darkness, Jesus
opened his small, bleating mouth (even before
his eyes widened to the supple world his
lungs had sighed into being), did he intuit
how hungrily the lungs gasp? Did he begin, then,
to love the way air sighs as it brushes in and out
through the portals of tissue to sustain
the tiny heart's iambic beating? And how,
fueled by air, the dazzling blood tramps
the crossroads of the brain like donkey tracks,
corpuscles skittering to the earlobes and toenails?

Bottle of the breath of God, speaking in stories,
shouting across wild, obedient water, his voice
was stoppered only by inquisition, unfaith
and anguish. Did he know that he would,
in the end, leak all his blood, heave a final
groan and throw his breath,
oxygen for the world, back to its Source
before the next dark cave?

Mary's Song

Blue homespun and the bend of my breast
keep warm this small hot naked star
fallen to my arms. (Rest . . .
you who have had so far to come.)
Now nearness satisfies
the body of God sweetly. Quiet he lies
whose vigor hurled a universe. He sleeps
whose eyelids have not closed before.

His breath (so slight it seems
no breath at all) once ruffled the dark deeps
to sprout a world. Charmed by doves' voices,
the whisper of straw, he dreams,
hearing no music from his other spheres.
Breath, mouth, ears, eyes,
he is curtailed who overflowed all skies,
all years. Older than eternity, now he
is new. Now native to earth as I am, nailed
to my poor planet, caught
that I might be free, blind in my womb
to know my darkness ended,
brought to this birth for me to be new-born,
and for him to see me mended,
I must see him torn.

Night's lodging

Across the purple-patterned snow
laced with light of lantern-glow,
dappled with dark,
comes Christ, the Child born from the skies.
Those are stars that are his eyes.
His baby face is wise
seen by my candle spark.
But is he cold from the wind's cold blow?
Where will he go?

I'll wrap him warm with love,
well as I'm able,
in my heart stable.

The groundhog

The groundhog is, at best, a simple soul
    without pretension, happy in his hole,
twinkle-eyed, shy, earthy, coarse-coated gray,
    of little use (except on Groundhog Day).
At Christmastime a rather doubtful fable
    gives the beast standing room inside the stable
with other simple things, shepherds, and sheep,
    cows, and small winter birds, and on the heap
of warm, sun-sweetened hay, the simplest thing
    of all — a Baby. Can a groundhog sing,
or only grunt his wonder? Could he know
    this new-born Child had planned him, long ago,
for groundhog-hood? Whether true tale or fable,
    I like to think that he *was* in the stable,
part of the Plan, and that He who designed
    all simple wonderers, may have had me in mind.

Presents

"Thanks be to God for his unspeakable gift."
2 Corinthians 9:15

What's so good as getting?
The anticipation, snow
in the air, people with lists,
voices that drop when you
enter the room, the pine-wood
fire smell and the smell of pine
needles from the trimmed tree
by the window — it all narrows down
to the heft of the package in the
hands, the wondering, the unwrapping
(Careful — the paper's too pretty
to tear), the oh, the ah. What's
so good as getting

if not giving?
The covert questions, the catalogs
with corners turned back, the love
that overlooks cost, the hiding place
in the hamper, the card whose
colored words can't say it all,
the glee of linking want/wish

with have/hold, the handing over,
fingers brushing, the thing
revealed, the spark as the eyes
meet, and the hug. What's
so good as giving?

Shine in the Dark

From a dark dust of stars
kindled one, a prick of light.
Burn! Small candle star,
burn in the black night.

In the still, hushed heart
(shadowed as a black night)
shine! Savior newly born,
shine till the heart's light.

Star Song

Glimmers from stars
have flickered all year long,
and now, at its close,
when the planets
are shining through frost,
radiance runs like music in the bones,
and the heart keeps rising
at the sound of any song,

or with the silver calling
of a bell,
rounding, high and clear,
flying, falling,
sounding the death knell
of our old year,
telling the new appearing
of Christ, our Morning Star.

Now, burst,
all our bell throats!
Toll, every clapper tongue!
Stun the still night!
Jesus himself gleams through
our high heart notes

(it is no fable).
It is he whose light
glistens in each song sung,
and in the true
returning again
to the stable
of all of us: shepherds,
sages, his women and men,
common and faithful,
wealthy and wise,
with carillon hearts,
and, suddenly, stars
in our eyes.

Living

Simeon

"You are to give to the Lord the firstborn of every womb."
Exodus 13:2, 12

"The Lord makes his life an offering for sin . . ."
Isaiah 53:10

Expectant, though never knowing quite
what he was watching for, the old man
had waited out the years of a long life
to be in the right place,
at the right time.

How many generations of crying babies
brought by new parents into the holy precincts
for dedication? How many innocent doves
wrung by the neck for their blood,
and burned on the altar? Yet, when *they*
came with their child and their pigeons,
and when the man Simeon, seized by Spirit,
took the infant in his arms, his eyes
looked into the eyes of God; there was
that flash of absolute knowing.

So, as the Law decreed, he gave the child
back to the Master of the Universe, singing
for joy (salvation now had come),
and grief (a sword was in his song).

Here was the fulfillment
of Simeon's expectation.
Here in the Presentation, he saw the
commencement of the Offering.

Madonna and Child, with Saints

Sandro Botticelli (1445-1510), Uffizi Museum, Firenze

Jesus looking like a real baby, not
a bony homunculus, solemn and all-knowing.
The quill in the hand of his newly minted mother
stretches toward the bottle of ink a beautiful boy saint
is holding out. He has waited for centuries for her
to write in a book the next words of her own Magnificat,
for the Gospel of St. Luke, and for us to sing in church.
Two other youths try to lower a crown onto her head.
It is too large for her, and they've held it there for so long,
but she seems bored with royalty, eyes only for
her son, and his for her. In her left hand, as she
supports the child, she holds a pomegranate
under his fingers for him to pluck, its red leather skin
peeled back to expose its packed rubies.
Centuries later the paint and the fruit are fresh
and tart as ever, glowing like blood cells.

I wonder about sound in the room — small talk among
the impossibly adolescent saints. Mary talking baby talk,
perhaps, or singing as if she has swallowed a linnet —
Mary with the pale green voice, nothing coloratura,
more like grapes glowing from a low trellis.

In the moist Italian twilight, a cricket is likely to be sawing
like the sawing of cedar boards in the work room just outside
the painting's frame — Joseph laboring on a baby bed.

But there isn't a bird or an insect. There is just this lovely girl,
waking to motherhood, humming, content, in this
moment in time, to be God's mother, to hold Jesus,
when he cries, to her leaking breast.

As Botticelli lifts with his skilled hand a fine brush
to add the next word to her song, we look with him
through the lens of his devotion, into this ornate room.
He paints love pouring through her skin like light,
her eyes resting on the child as though
he is all there is, as though her knowing will never
be complete. Right from the beginning
"How can this be?" circles her mind with its echo.

Bluff Edge, Whidbey Island

This is the rock-rim edge of the known world.
This is the ragged planet where Christ landed,
and we are his people, craggy and knotted and burled,
and aching and lonely. Restless. Stranded.

These firs could well have framed his wooden manger
and his cross; I never encounter Advent without
Dark Friday. The days in the life of this stranger
were flecked with God-graces, threaded with human doubt.

Battered by storms of loss in her loving and grieving,
all her life Mary lived on the cliff-edge of cruel foresight.
Clinging, she rode the gusts and the glory, heaving
still with the donkey rhythm, dazzled with western light.

At the Cloisters

On the stone wall, in shadow,
Madonna and Child, with the Child
gone. Bearing the baby
she'd lately borne — cradling him
who upholds the whole, heavy world —
stands Mary, fractured by
an unbearable gravity not
her own. It must be that pull,
and the violence of time,
that has broken her hands off
at the wrists.

Through blank air, past
the small, missing face,
she catches my eye. We exchange
a wry secret: our common breakage
mends the gap of years as we both
let our children go, and learn
the start of weight loss —
its holy levity. Oh!

December 15

Out in the county, on the way up to the pass,
we found the tree farm, chose a U-cut tree from
a cluster of others under the brow of a hill. We sawed it
down, our ungloved fingers bone-cold, roped it,
dragged it across a wide pasture's worth of stubble
and thin snow. Home then, stump jutting awkwardly
out the tailgate for the bumpy, unfamiliar journey into town.

We propped it on the back deck in its water pail, where
it waited for us to be ready for it. That week we moved
the red chair away from the window, set up the tree stand,
cloved cider simmering on the stove, the *Messiah* playing
in the background, boxed ornaments cluttering
the floor. The exchange! From hilly silence, biting air,
an immense white sky, to our house and our smug interior.

Once we'd raised it, fingers tingling from needles
and sticky with resin, how central it looked, there
in the living room, lit with its strings of light,
its treasures from the attic and the years! Also, somehow,
surprising, but never as astonishing as the one
come from heaven to be lifted up, drawing us all back to
his rude end, his singular, green life, the festal forests,
the wide fields and hills and sky of his beginning.

Jordan River

Naaman went down seven times.
Imagine it — the leprous skin coming
clear and soft, and the heart too.
But can you vision clean Jesus
under Jordan's water? John the Baptizer did,
holding the thin white body down,
seeing it muddied as any sinner's
against river bottom, grimed by
the ground of his being.

Rising then, he surfaced, a sudden
fountain. But who would have expected
that thunderclap, the explosion of light
as the sky fell, the Spirit seizing him,
violent, a whir of winged light and sound
witnessing his work, his worth,
shaking him until the drops
flew from his shoulders, wet and common
and holy, Baptized sprinkling baptizer.

"He who would be great among you . . ."

Matthew 20:26

You, whose birth broke all the social and biological rules —
son of the poor who was worshiped as a king —
you were the kind who used a new math to multiply
bread, fish, faith. You practiced a radical sociology:
rehabilitating call girls and con men.
You valued women and other minority groups.
A family practitioner, you specialized in heart transplants.

Creator, healer, shepherd, storyteller,
innovator, weather-maker, exorcist, iconoclast,
seeker, seer, motive-sifter, you were always beyond, above us,
ahead of your time, and ours.
And we would like to be like you!
Bold as the Boanerges we hear ourselves demand:
"Admit us to your inner circle.
Grant us degree in all the liberal arts of heaven."

Why our belligerence? Why does this whiff of fame
and power smell so sweet?
Why must we compete
to be first? Have we forgotten
how you took, so simply, cool water
and a towel for our feet?

Royalty

He was a plain man
and learned no latin.

Having left all gold behind
he dealt out peace
to all us wild ones
and the weather.

He ate fish, bread,
country wine and God's will.

Dust sandaled his feet.

He wore purple only once
and that was an irony.

Odd couples

Things are so often
at odds with their containers.

Our cat once nested her young
in a bureau drawer.

The copper kettle on the shelf
is boiling with partridge berries.

Other mixed metaphors rush
to be recognized:

That baby in the corncrib.
God in a sweaty carpenter's body.

Eternity spilled the third day
from a hole in the hill

for you, a painter-plumber,
me, a poet sorting socks,

all of us teetotalers drunk
on the Holy Ghost.

Look!

As we learned how to read,
were we beginning to forget to look,
our young eyes caught in tangles of print
so that imagination was choked? Were we
trapped at that remove from ourselves?

Or did we begin to see a new way, with eyes
that widened in the amazement of reverie,
memory, invention? As we peered
between the words, could we make out
shapes and colors beyond them?

What did our inside eyes make of
the black marks on creamy paper, on onionskin?
A dream of angels turned real, perhaps.
A wooden boat on a lake. Three small loaves
fragmented to fill all those empty mouths

and baskets. Or this: a blind man
opening his eyes so that the first face he sees —
a vision, surely — is Christ's, spittle
still shining on the quick fingers,
his mouth saying urgently, *Look!*

Flathead Lake, Montana

"Christ plays in ten thousand places."
Gerard Manley Hopkins

Lying here on the short grass, I am
a bowl for sunlight.

Silence. A bee. The lip lip of water
over stones. The swish and slap, hollow

under the dock. Down-shore
a man sawing wood.

Christ in the sunshine laughing
through the green translucent wings

of maple seeds. A bird
resting its song on two notes.

Dying

The Revolutionary

Do you wince when
you hear his name
made vanity?

What if you were not so safe,
sheltered, circled by love
and tradition? What if
the world shouted at you?
Could you take the string of
hoarse words — glutton, wino,
devil, crazy man, agitator, bastard,
nigger-lover, rebel —
and hang the grimy ornament
around your neck
and answer *love*?

See the sharp stones poised
against your head! Even
your dear friend
couples your name with curses
("By God, I know not God!").
The obscene affirmation
of infidelity

echoes, insistent,
from a henhouse roof.

Then, Slap! Spit! The whip,
the thorn. The gravel
grinds your fallen knees
under a whole world's weight
until the hammering home
of all your virtue
stakes you, stranded,
halfway between hilltop
and heaven (neither will
have you).

And will you whisper
forgive?

Son and Mother

How many nails pierced the cross's wood?
Four.
One and one for the hands outspread,
Bone and tendon and flesh blood red.
For feet, one. One for the sign above his head.
Four to the strength of the heartwood tore.
Four.

How many thorns crowned Messiah's brow?
Ten.
Each like the tooth of an angry plow,
From which ten blooms of bright blood grew.
The color of death and of debt long due
Canceled with ink from God's own pen.
Ten.

How many swords stabbed Mary's heart?
One.
The cry from the cross was its sharpest dart.
She'd pondered the pain from the very start
Till it grew to a lifelong ache. The hurt
Weighed huge and chill as a burying stone —
One.

Bread turned to stone: Pietà

Her polished, sculpted arm supports
the marble son, the eyes of Mary
and Jesus both sightless, mouths dumb,
ears sealed to sound, fingers frozen in place.
No hearts under the carved cloth
to pulse and turn again to flesh,
fulfilling Ezekiel. How permanent
is this paralysis? When should we expect
the miracle? How will stone become bread,
become living Word again?

A bird in the church

The black bird, not caught like us at
one lowly level, has entered this
stone cage of a church
with its fluidities of enclosed light.

Between crossbeam and cornice, wide
and high and low and up again, through
the sun's transfixing shafts, her wings
open and close in a bewilderment

of interior air, until, homing,
she glides down the path of light
behind the altar, and settles
high on the arm of the crucifix.

Having found a nesting tree,
she lodges at last where vertex
and horizon meet, resting in
the steady love of Christ's left eye.

Angel Vision

"There are things into which angels long to look."
1 Peter 1:12

Seeing Creation come, they know it well:
the stars, the shoots of green shine for them
one by one. They have eternity to learn
the universe, which, once encompassing,
angels forget not. Clean as steel wires, shining
as frost, making holiness beautiful, aiming
at the Will of God like arrows flaming
to a target, earthly solidity presents no
barrier to their going. Easily they slope
through the rind of the world, the atoms
pinging in their celestial orifices.
Inhabiting the purposes of God, Who is
the Lord of all their Hosts, on Earth and in
Deep Space, their congregation wages war
against the Hierarchies of Darkness
with swords of fire and power and great joy.
The rising Day Star is their standard bearer,
as on earth they stay the Adversary's slaughter
of God's radiant sons and daughters.

      Praise
is their delight also. Rank on rank they sing
circularly around the Throne, dancing together

in a glory, clapping joyful hands at all rebellion
repented of, or lost sheep found. They who
accompany the lifting of a redeemed swimmer
from the final wave, who trace the pathway of
the unrepentant one to his own place —
how can we think to escape their fiery ministry?
We listen for their feathers, missing the shaft of light
at our own shoulder. We tread our gauntlet paths
unknowing, covered by shields of angels.

     Seraphim sing in no time zone. Cherubim see
as clearly on as back, invest acacia wood with arkhood
in their certainty; their winged ornamentation
gilds the tabernacle shade. Comprehending the
compacted plan centered in every seed, the grown
plant is no more real to them, and no surprise.
Dampened by neither doubt nor supposition,
the archangel sees with eyes sharper than ours.
For him, reality's seemingly random choice is all clear
Cause and Effect: each star of snow tells of intelligence;
each cell carries its own code; at a glance each angel
knows from whence the crests of all the wrinkles on
the sea rebound. He has eternity to tell it all,
and to rejoice.

     But here and now, in Judea, what is
this scandal of particularity? This conjunction of straw
and splendor? Of deity and agony? The echo of

sharp laughter from a crowd, as hammered nails pierce flesh,
pierces the Bright Ones with perplexity. They see
the Maker's hands helpless against Made Wood.
The bond is sealed with God's blood, the body buried.
In this is Love's substance become darkness
to their light. The Third Day sweetens the mystery.
Astonished heralds now of Resurrection,
they have eternity to solve it, and to praise.

The Partaking

Bread of the Presence
was, in Moses' day,
served on engraved gold plates
to you and your select few.
And in exclusive glory
one alone and lonely man
sprinkled, with fear,
the ceremonial drops that pleaded
failure for another year
to you, known then
as only high and holy —
heavens apart from common
women, common men.

Often we taste the
granular body of wheat
(Think of the Grain that was buried
and died!)
and swallow together
the grape's warm, burning blood
(Remembering First Fruit!)
knowing ourselves a part of you
as you took part of us, flowed
in our kind of veins,

quickened cells like ours
into a human subdividing:
now you are multiplied —
we are your fingers and your feet,
your tender heart — we
are your broken side.

Take now, and crumble small,
and cast our human flesh on
the world's waters, your contemporary
Shewbread. Feed us
to more than five thousand women and men,
and in our dark, daily flood of living
pour yourself out again.

Craftsman

Carpenter's son, carpenter's son,
is the wood fine and smoothly sanded,
or rough-grained, lying along your back?
Was it well-planed? Did they use
a plumb line when they set you up?
Is the angle true? Why did they choose
such dark, expensive stain
to gloss the timbers next to your feet
and fingers? You should know, who,
Joseph-trained, judged all trees
for special service.

Carpenter's son, carpenter's son,
were the nails new and cleanly driven
when the dark hammers sang?
Is the earth warped from where you hang,
high enough for a world view?

Carpenter's son, carpenter's son,
was it a job well done?

Evergreen

Topped
with an earthbound angel,
burdened
with man-made stars,
tinsel-draped,
but touched with no
true gold,
cropped, girdled
with electricity —
why be
a temporary tree,
glass-fruited, dry,
uprooted?

When you may be
planted with purpose
in a flowered field,
and where,
living in clean light,
strong air,
crowned with
the repeated gold
of every evening,
every night

real stars may nest
in your elbow,
rest
be found in your shade,
healing
in your perennial green,
and from deep springs your roots
may suck enough to swell
within you
the Spirit's sweetest fruits.

Cross, Holy Week

On my chest this Friday afternoon,
the elegant small signature
of violent death
swings on my neck as I walk,
gold tapping my deep heart,
telling me I was there.
*(I did not mean to do it; I did
not know.)* I slump under
the weight of it; my pulse
echoes the beat of hammers.

Onlookers

"Sickness and dying are places . . . where
there's no company, where nobody can follow."
Flannery O'Connor

Behind our shield of health, each
of us must sense another's anguish
secondhand; we are agnostic
in the face of birth and dying. So Joseph felt,
observer of the push and splash of entry,
and Mary, under the cross's arm.

Only their son, and God's,
in bearing all our griefs,
felt them firsthand, climbing
himself our rugged hill of pain.
His nerves, enfleshed, carried
the messages of nails, the tomb's
chill. His ever-open wounds still
blazon back to us all the pack of pain
we didn't have to bear, and heaven
gleams for us more real,
crossed with his human blood.

Perfect Christmas Tree

Jesus Evergreen, from top to toe
your springy boughs are hung
with surprise — a gift here, a gift
there — wreathed with a glitter
of graces, all your needles
lacy with air and the remembrance
of small snow, your freshness
filling the house with the festal
smell of the forest. Your tough
length has bent to the wind, the ax,
but now the centering trunk
lances straight up, piercing
your slow green dying with the ache
of being felled. While the rooted
mountain spruces sing, resin
bleeds from your cut heart.

Trauma center

It was never meant
to burst from the body
so fiercely, to pour
unchanneled from
the five wounds
and the unbandaged brow,
drowning the dark wood,
staining the stones
and the dust below,
clotting in the air
dark with God's absence.

It was created for
a closed system —
the unbroken rhythms
of human blood
binding the body
of God, circulating
hot, brilliant,
saline, without
interruption
between heart, lungs,
and all cells.

But because he
was once emptied,
I am each day refilled;
my spirit-arteries
pulse with the vital red
of love; poured out,
it is his life that now
pumps through
my own heart's core.
He bled, and died, and I
have been transfused.

Risen

". . . for they shall see God"

Matthew 5:8

Christ risen was rarely
recognized by sight.
They had to get beyond the way he looked.
Evidence stronger than
his voice and face and footstep
waited to grow in them, to guide
their groping from despair,
their stretching toward belief.

We are as blind as they
until the opening of our deeper eyes
shows us the hands that bless
and break our bread,
until we finger
wounds that tell our healing,
or witness a miracle of fish
dawn-caught after our long night
of empty nets. Handling
his Word, we feel his flesh,
his bones, and hear his voice
calling our early-morning name.

Open

John 20:19, 26

Doubt padlocked one door and
Memory put her back to the other.
Still the damp draught seeped in, though
Fear chinked all the cracks and
Blindness boarded up the window.
In the darkness that was left
Defeat crouched, shivering,
in his cold corner.

Then Jesus came
(all the doors being shut)
and stood among them.

Fraction

Like the winter morning ice that,
beautiful and brittle, skins a puddle —

like the wafer the priest lifts and snaps
with the fingers of his two hands —

a pistol shot across the congregation —
so is the name of Jesus splintered

to fall in fragments from our tongues,
sharpening the oath-speech

of the careless, feeding others
with light from the broken crystal.

Galilee, Easter Day

Quietly the old lake
leans against the land,
rubbing a shoulder
along the pebbles, water-worn,
sun-warm. The lips of the ripples
mouth old secrets. Their edges
lend the shore a small silver. Stolid,
the gray stones move a little
in the glancing light.

But we, waiting for
the Great Appearing, will we
listen and learn — we who gingerly
walk the rough border
where he walked?
Ankle-deep in water lapping
over the boulders, sharp, hot
in the sun, can we feel with our feet
the narrow margin
and sense the need to stand
firm, without retreat to the path
worn smooth by passing tourists?
Why do we gaze down,
still searching for footholds?
When will we be ready
to look up, to rise at the call
of the rising Light?

Getting inside the miracle

No, he is too quick. We never
catch him at it. He is there
sooner than our thought or prayer.
Searching backward, we cannot discover
how, or get inside the miracle.

Even if it were here and now
how would we describe the just-born trees
swimming into place at their green
creation, flowering upward in the air
with all their thin twigs quivering
in the gusts of grace? Or the great
white whales fluking through
crystalline seas like recently inflated
balloons? Who could time the beat
of the man's heart as the woman
comes close enough to fill
his newly hollow side? Who will diagram
the gynecology of Incarnation,
the trigonometry of Trinity?
Or chemically analyze wine from a well?
Or see inside joints as they loosen,
and whole limbs, and lives? Will anyone
stand beside the moving stone? And plot

the bright trajectory of Ascension?
And explain the tongues of fire
telling both heat and light?

Enough. Refrain. Observe
a finished work. Think —
today, another miracle: the feathered
arrows of my faith may link
God's bow and target.

The labors of angels

Upon seeing the painting by Roger Wagner, The Harvest
Is the End of the World and the Reapers Are Angels

Plucking our meager treasures, grain
by grain, we disregard celestial messengers
to our jeopardy.

Sexless and muscular, angels
must wrestle, pitting light against
sinew and darkness. They arrive
without notice, blazing, terrifying us
with good news.

Barren or virgin
we bear our improbable children
and angels raise heaven like a song.
Still, angels can weep;
in your mind's eye, see
their clear, mineral tears.

Against the indigo sky,
where judgment pulses
like an aneurysm, sunlight spins
its horizontal threads across the field until

the yellows in the standing wheat stalks
match the low light. Harvester angels
cast huge wings of shadow,
scything a crop, lifting it
from the skin of an acre
like fleece from a sheep's flank.

It is only later that they delicately
unhook teasel, thistle, burdock
from the heavy gold grain.

Rising: The Underground Tree

(Cornus sanguinea and *cornus canadensis)*

One spring in Tennessee I walked a tunnel
under dogwood trees, noting the petals
(in fours like crosses) and at each tender apex
four russet stains dark as Christ-wounds.
I knew that with the year the dogwood flower heads
would ripen into berry clusters bright as drops of gore.

Last week, a double-click on Botany
startled me with the kinship of those trees
and bunchberries, whose densely crowded mat
carpets the deep woods around my valley cabin.
Only their flowers — those white quartets of petals —
suggest the blood relationship. Since then I see

the miniature leaves and buds as tips of trees
burgeoning underground, knotted roots like limbs
pushing up to light through rock and humus.
The pure cross-flowers at my feet redeem
their long, dark burial in the ground, show how even
a weight of stony soil cannot keep Easter at bay.

Judas, Peter

Because we are all
betrayers, taking
silver, and eating
body and blood, and asking
(guilty) is it I, and hearing
him say yes,
it would be simple for us all
to rush out

and hang ourselves.

But if we find grace
to cry and wait
after the voice of morning
has crowed in our ears
clearly enough
to break our hearts,
he will be there
to ask us each, again,
do you love me?

Highway Song for Valentine's Day

"Kim, I love you — Danny"
    roadside graffito

On overhead and underpass,
beside the road, beyond the grass,

in aerosol or paint or chalk
the stones cry out, the billboards talk.

On rock and wall and bridge and tree,
boldly engraved for all to see,

hearts and initials intertwine
their passionate, short-lived valentine.

I'm listening for a longer Lover
whose declaration lasts forever:

from field and flower, through wind and breath,
in straw and star, by birth and death,

his urgent language of desire
flickers in dew and frost and fire.

This earliest spring that I have seen
shows me that tender love in green,

and on my windshield, clear and plain,
my Dearest signs his name in rain.

Seed

God dug his seed
into dry, dark earth.
After a sprouting up
in hopeful birth
and healing bloom
and garland grace,
he buried it again
in a darker place.

Twice rudely planted seed,
root, rise in me
and grow your green again,
your fruited tree.

Spring, St. Martin's Chapel: Cathedral of St. John the Divine

for Madeleine L'Engle

Both of us kneel, then wait
on the church chairs — square, chocolate brown —
knowing that soon the black priest

will hurry in, wearing his lateness like
the wrong robe. In the pregnant emptiness
before communion, that crack between worlds,

we listen inward, feet tight on the cold slate,
wanting to hear Christ tell us *Feed on me.*
Our hearts shiver, hidden. Nothing visible moves.

Outside a drizzle starts; drops spit on the sill.
The window bird flies motionless in
a cobalt sky of skillful glass.

But beyond the frame, plucking the eye
like a message from Outside, a minor shadow
tilts and swoops in light rain,

wings telling us to fly wide, loose
and nervy as sparrows who may peck crumbs from
any picnic table, or gnats right out of the air.

The Golden Ratio & the Coriolis Force*

This morning God himself — his wafer —
lay for a moment naked on my tongue.
I felt the blood of God race through my veins.
Week by week Christ's flesh gets
broken down in my own body cells, as
the platelets in my plasma, like an uncurling
swirl of skyward birds, like my life spiral,
maintain their swift unwinding.

The second law.

The hurricanes, like commas
on the weather map. Amoebas.
Waterspouts. Curled fetuses.
Convolvulus vines twisting anti-clockwise
on the trellis. Dust devils dancing over fields.
The spiral nebulae. The nautilus.
The human ear. The bathtub water
scrolling down the drain — everything
made by God looks God-like,
and these unfolding spirals seem to me

*The Coriolis force describes how moving objects, such as water going down a
drain, are deflected as a result of the earth's rotation, spiraling right in the north-
ern hemisphere and left in the southern hemisphere.

the shape of God. The universe, once
wound up, is now rewinding, like my life —
to zero and the Everything of God
(who lay this morning naked
on the manger of my tongue).

Two stanzas: The Eucharist

Annie Dillard speaks of Christ
corked in a bottle: carrying the wine
to Communion in a pack on her back,
she feels him lambent, lighting
the hidden valleys through the spaces
between her ribs. Nor can we
contain him in a cup. He is always
poured out for our congregation.
And see how he spills, hot, light,
his oceans glowing like wine,
flooding all the fjords among
the bones of our continents.

Annie Dillard once asked: How
in the world can we *remember* God?
(Death forgets and we all die.)
But truly, reminders are God's
business. He will see to it,
flashing his parts, now,
then, past our cut in the rock.
His metaphors are many, among them
the provided feast by which
our teeth and tongues and throats
hint to our hearts of God's body,
giving us the *why* of Incarnation,
the *how* of remembrance.

Step on it

All these broken bridges —
we have always tried to build them
to each other and
to heaven. Why is it such a sad
surprise when last year's iron-strong,
out-thrust organization, this month's
shining project, today's silver network
of good resolutions
all answer the future's questions with
rust, and the sharp, ugly jutting
of the unfinished?
We have miscalculated every time.
Our blueprints are smudged.
We never order enough steel.
Our foundations are shallow as mud.
Our cables fray. Our superstructure
is stuck together clumsily
with rivets of the wrong size.

We are our own botched bridges.
We were schooled in Babel,
and our ambitious soaring
sinks in the sea. How could we ever
hope to carry your heavy glory?

We cannot even bear the weight
of our own failure.

But you did the unthinkable.
You built one Bridge to us,
solid enough, long enough,
strong enough to stand all tides
for all time, linking
the unlinkable.

Sensing

St. Paul's Episcopal Church, Bellingham

A bloom like phosphorescence shines on
the newel posts at the ends of the pews. Is it the candles
standing on the altar, fat and white as milk,
with their heads on fire — vowels of light? Is it

the winter sun bleeding through stained glass
so that our faces begin to burn like lanterns?
Is it the air, with its brew of scents: varnished wood,
heat from the old radiators, and a whiff of consecrated oil?

There's the salt of old sweat, a profligacy of spice —
pungent distress and quandary and creed.
The seed of faith being sown again and again,
the fragrance of psalms, and their ancient verbal music.

The brassy cross in procession, an organ flourish,
and kneelers that creak when we slump down, confessing.
Gospel words from the aisle and the pulpit, the tread
of steps up to the altar, shriven souls inhaling,

hands and lips lifted for food and drink, the giving and taking
of ourselves — the commerce of heaven. Perhaps it's a kind
of incense just to be *this* — the prosaic body of God with peace
and grace passed among us, and a few crimson choir robes.

To Know Him Risen

Is it obliquely
    through time's telescope, thick-
    lensed with two thousand Easters?
Or to my ear in Latin, three chanted
    Kyries triumphing over a purple chancel?
Or in a rectangular glance at sepia snapshots
    of Jerusalem's Historic Sites?
Can I touch him through the cliché crust
    of lilies, stained glass, sunrise services?
Is a symbol soluble?
Can I flush out my eyes and rinse away
    the scales?
Must I be there?
Must I feel his freshness
    at an interval of inches? And sense,
    incredulous, the reassurance of warm breath?
    And hear again the grit of stone
    under his sandal sole?
    Those familiar vowels
    in the deep voicing of beatitude? Recognize
    the straight stance, quick eye,
    strength, purpose, movement, clear command —
    all the swift three-day antonyms of death
    that spring up to dispel its sting,
    to contradict its loss?
Must I be Thomas, belligerent in doubt,

hesitant, tentative, convinced, humbled, loved,
and *there?*
Must sight sustain belief?
Or is a closer blessedness
to know him risen — now,
in this moment's finger-thrust of faith — here,
as an inner eye perceives?

Acknowledgments

Grateful acknowledgment is made to the editors of the following publications, in which some of these poems have most recently appeared:

Crux: "Simeon"

Image: "Madonna and Child, with Saints"

Weavings: "Descent"

The poems "Advent Visitation," "Magnificat," "One," and "The labors of angels" were published in *The Angles of Light* (Shaw/Waterbrook, 2000).

The poems "Highway Song for Valentine's Day," "I gave this day to God," and "Rising: The Underground Tree" were published in *The Green Earth* (William B. Eerdmans, 2002).

The poems "Angel Vision," "Announcement," "Craftsman," "Evergreen," ". . . for they shall see God," ". . . for who can endure the day of his coming?" "Galilee, Easter Day," "Getting inside the miracle," "The groundhog," "Jordan River," "Judas, Peter," "He who would be great among you . . . ," "Made Flesh," "Mary's Song," "Major Theme to a Minor Tune," "The Meaning of White Oaks," "Night's lodging," "Odd couples," "Onlookers," "Open," "The Partaking," "Presents," "The Revolutionary," "Royalty," "Salutation," "Seed," "Shine in the dark," "Christmas stars," "Son and Mother," "Step on it," "To Know Him Risen," "Too Much to Ask," "Two stanzas: The Eucharist," and "Trauma center" were published in *Polishing the Petoskey Stone* (Regent College Publishing, 2003).

The poem "Star Song" was published in *The Sighting* (Shaw, 1978).

The poems "Bluff Edge, Whidbey Island," "Flathead Lake, Montana," "Fraction," "The Golden Ratio & the Coriolis Force," "Look!" and "Spring, St. Martin's Chapel" were published in *Water Lines* (William B. Eerdmans, 2003).

The poems "At the Cloisters," "The Overshadow," "Virgin," "A bird in the church," "Cross, Holy Week," and "Perfect Christmas Tree" were published in *Writing the River* (Regent College Publishing, 1998).